THE CIA

The CIA witnessed the execution of Cuban revolutionary Che Guevara in 1967.

THE CIA

ODYSSEYS

KRISSY EBERTH

CREATIVE EDUCATION · CREATIVE PAPERBACKS

Published by Creative Education and Creative Paperbacks
P.O. Box 227, Mankato, Minnesota 56002
Creative Education and Creative Paperbacks
are imprints of The Creative Company
www.thecreativecompany.us

Design by Graham Morgan
Art direction by Tom Morgan
Edited by Jill Kalz

Images by Alamy Stock Photo/Atlaspix, 24, LaPresse, 66, VIEMOSE K•RE, 27; Associated Press/Denis Paquin, 54; Getty Images/gorodenkoff, 31, Hulton Deutsch, 41, Keystone, 12, Keystone-France, 8, Libkos, 73, Mark Wilson, 38, New York Times Co., 20, Viaframe, 6; INA FASSBENDER/Reuters, cover, 37; NASA, 46; Pexels/Brett Sayles, 28; Public Domain/U.S. Army, 11; Wikimedia Commons/Askild Antonsen, 4-5, CIA, 34-35, Claude Salhani, 57, Emanuel Leutze/The Metropolitan Museum of Art, 14, Gustavo Villoldo, CIA operative, 2, PatrickCaproni, 50, public domain, 52, Sajjad Ali Qureshi, 70-71, Tiomono, 60, U.S. federal government, 63, U.S. Space Force photo by Tech. Sgt. Luke Kitterman, 48, Underwood & Underwood, 19

Every effort has been made to contact copyright holders for material reproduced in this book. Any omissions will be rectified in subsequent printings if notice is given to the publisher.

Copyright © 2025 Creative Education, Creative Paperbacks
International copyright reserved in all countries. No part of this book may be reproduced in any form without written permission from the publisher.

Library of Congress Cataloging-in-Publication Data
Names: Eberth, Krissy, author.
Title: The CIA / Krissy Eberth.
Description: Mankato, Minnesota : Creative Education and Creative Paperbacks, [2025] | Series: Odysseys in spycraft | Includes bibliographical references and index. | Audience: Ages 12-15 | Audience: Grades 7-9 | Summary: "Unlock the spy secrets of the United States' Central Intelligence Agency (CIA), from the American espionage agency's history to counterterrorism training and key missions. Includes a glossary, sidebars, index, and further resources"— Provided by publisher.
Identifiers: LCCN 2024018510 (print) | LCCN 2024018511 (ebook) | ISBN 9798889892939 (library binding) | ISBN 9781682776599 (paperback) | ISBN 9798889894049 (ebook)
Subjects: LCSH: United States. Central Intelligence Agency—Juvenile literature. | Intelligence service—United States—Juvenile literature. | Secret service—United States—Juvenile literature.
Classification: LCC JK468.I6 E28 2025 (print) | LCC JK468.I6 (ebook) | DDC 327.1273—dc23/eng/20240503
LC record available at https://lccn.loc.gov/2024018510
LC ebook record available at https://lccn.loc.gov/2024018511

Printed in the United States of America

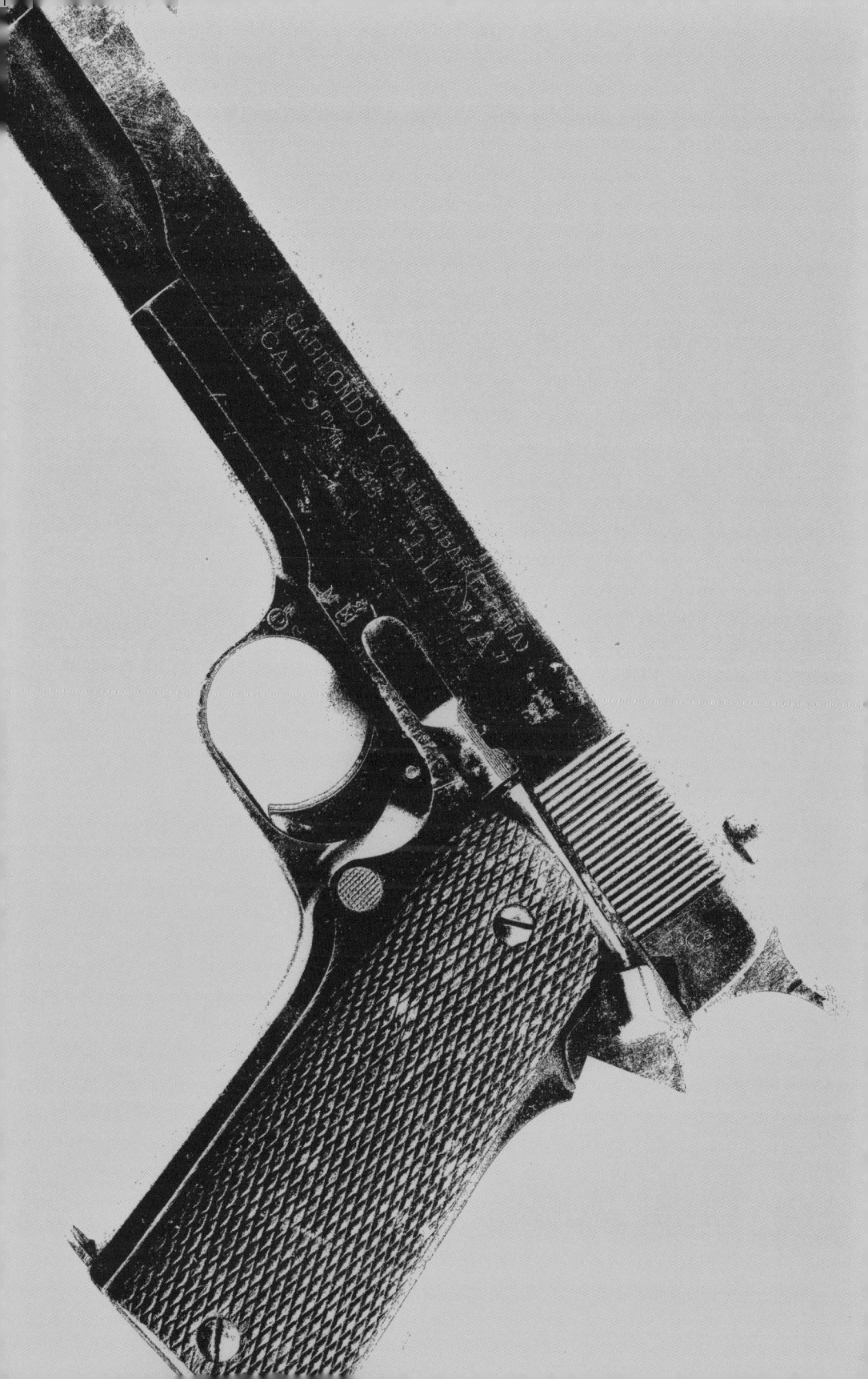

Remotely piloted drones are efficient tools for spying from above.

CONTENTS

Introduction 9

Founding and Origins 15

OSS All-Stars 20

Fact vs. Fiction 25

MICE 28

On the Big Screen 35

Tools and Tricks 39

Failure in the Sky 41

Notable Agents 51

On a Mission 61

CIA Seal 63

The Hunt Ends 70

Selected Bibliography 76

Glossary 77

Websites 79

Index 80

THE CIA

Introduction

Long ago, Chinese soldier and philosopher Sun Tzu wrote, "All warfare is based on deception." He meant that a nation can't win a war without deceiving its enemies in some way or uncovering secret information its enemies don't want revealed. Spying, or gathering **intelligence**, is something all countries do, including the United States. It's necessary for national security.

OPPOSITE: Spies in the 1960s used an assortment of gadgets and media to gather information.

People often associate spying with dropping in and working behind enemy lines. But that's not always the case.

In 1970, the best-known manufacturer of **cipher** machines was a Swiss company called Crypto AG. It had militaries and governments all around the world as clients. The United States and West Germany secretly purchased the company and hid ownership from everyone, even the employees. The secret purchase gave the Central Intelligence Agency (CIA), which gathers foreign intelligence for the United States, access to Crypto AG's global portfolio. This included Egypt, Argentina,

In the 1930s, polygraph machines were a relatively new form of testing a person's truthfulness.

"MOST PEOPLE IN WASHINGTON, D.C., SIMPLY CALL [THE CIA] 'THE COMPANY.'"

Greece, Italy, India, Iran, and more than 50 other countries. The CIA and German intelligence changed a mechanism in their cipher machines. Using code name "Operation Rubicon," they made the mechanism insecure, allowing it to be read by them. Rubicon is considered one of the most successful intelligence thefts—and the most successful CIA operation—of the 20th century, due to the amount of highly sensitive information it collected. It allowed the United States and West Germany to spy on their enemies for decades. It was a feast of intelligence.

Founding and Origins

Today's CIA has its roots in the early 1900s, when the first official American intelligence agency was created. In 1908, the U.S. Justice Department established the Bureau of Information. In 1935, the agency's name was changed to the Federal Bureau of Investigation (FBI). The FBI is still the nation's main weapon against **counterespionage** within the United States.

OPPOSITE: General George Washington, who would later become the first president of the United States, made use of spies and intelligence during the Revolutionary War (1775–83).

As the world began moving toward World War II (1939–45), the Signal Intelligence Service (SIS) was established to intercept and read communications sent by radio, telegraph, or telephone between Germany or Japan and their allies. This work often required breaking complex codes used to keep messages secret. SIS agents achieved a major feat in 1940 by breaking the code used by Japanese government officials. They even intercepted a message just before December 7, 1941, revealing that Japan intended to attack the U.S. naval base at Pearl Harbor, Hawaii. Unfortunately, a breakdown in communications delayed sending out an alert before the actual attack began. After the United States entered World War II, the SIS greatly expanded its staff, going from 331 employees in 1941 to more than 10,000 by 1945.

While the SIS kept busy during World War II solving coded enemy messages, the FBI was focused on uncovering spy operations within the United States. Several pro-German and pro-Japanese spy rings were broken up, often with the help of **moles** or **double agents**. The FBI took on another key mission during the **Cold War** (1947–91): identifying Americans spying for the Soviet Union.

n 1942, an entirely new intelligence agency was born—the Office of Strategic Services (OSS). Organized by William "Wild Bill" Donovan, a

THE CIA

World War I (1914–18) combat hero and intelligence expert, the OSS carried out **covert** operations to support the United States and its allies during World War II. Donovan's nickname was fitting; he was always coming up with wild ideas. Once, he even proposed using bats to drop firebombs on Japan! Under Donovan's direction, OSS agents landed behind enemy lines to gather intelligence needed by army and navy units. They also smuggled supplies and **recruited** German and Japanese citizens to spy on their own countries.

After World War II ended in 1945, U.S. president Harry Truman wanted to disband the OSS. However, Donovan changed Truman's mind by outlining the threats posed by the emerging power of the Soviet Union. In 1947, the OSS was renamed the Central Intelligence Agency (CIA).

Intelligence expert William "Wild Bill" Donovan

Julia Child

OSS All-Stars

During World War II, "Wild Bill" Donovan brought together an unusual group of spies and challenged them to find creative ways of undermining Germany and Japan. Among those recruited for the Office of Strategic Services (OSS) were Hollywood directors John Ford and Merian Cooper, future expert chef Julia Child, and major-league baseball catcher Moe Berg. Ford and Cooper made films to sway public opinion against U.S. enemies. Child helped develop a shark repellent used by OSS divers attempting to damage or destroy German submarines. Berg, who could speak seven languages, was sent abroad to scope out secrets and assess the loyalties of foreign leaders.

The CIA is an independent agency that reports directly to the president. It has become the principal American intelligence agency acting outside the country. Most people in Washington, D.C., simply call it "The Company."

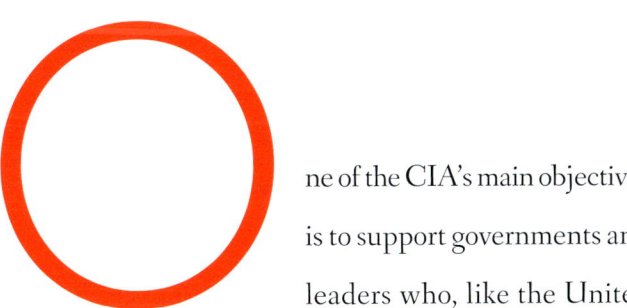

One of the CIA's main objectives is to support governments and leaders who, like the United States, oppose **communism** and terrorism. It also works to undermine governments that may pose a threat to

"OPERATING IN SECRECY, CIA AGENTS SELDOM RECEIVE RECOGNITION FOR THEIR ACCOMPLISHMENTS."

U.S. interests and security. The CIA carries out its work through four divisions: (1) the National **Clandestine** Service, or NCS (spies operating in the field); (2) the Directorate of Science and Technology (creators of special gadgets used by spies and instruments such as satellites, spy planes, cameras, and bugs); (3) the Directorate of Intelligence (information analysts); and

(4) the Directorate of Support (those responsible for training, supplies, and security, including such tasks as weeding out moles and double agents working inside the CIA itself). Only about 10 percent of the CIA's employees are actual spies.

While most of its employees live and work near the agency's headquarters in the Washington suburb of Langley, Virginia, the NCS division maintains stations in other countries. Their job is to analyze foreign political and military developments, recruit local people to provide intelligence, and determine if covert action needs to be taken to protect American interests. Operating in secrecy, CIA agents seldom receive recognition for their accomplishments. They do, however, sometimes get criticized for acting recklessly or breaking other countries' laws.

THE CIA

Fact vs. Fiction

Spies on television and in the movies often lead glamorous lives, wear cool disguises, and are usually attractive. Think Ethan Hunt of the *Mission: Impossible* movies or Jason Bourne of the Bourne franchise. In real life, **espionage** agencies such as the CIA recruit average-looking people who can blend in with others around them. In spy talk, the ability to blend in is called "going gray." Gray doesn't stand out the way bright colors do.

OPPOSITE: Matt Damon has played Jason Bourne in four movies, including 2016's *Jason Bourne*.

Despite what's portrayed in movies, only a small percentage of CIA agents do undercover spy work themselves. Some **operatives** use top secret tools and weapons to collect information or to carry out covert actions against foreigners who pose a threat to the United States. Most CIA agents, however, spend their time recruiting others in their station areas to gather intelligence. They take on the role of handler.

To survive in the field, a CIA agent needs a good legend, or cover story. The legend answers the questions

Born in Denmark, Morten Storm worked as a double agent for the CIA within the terrorist organization Al-Qaeda.

MICE

According to American journalist and espionage expert Ernest Volkman, the reasons people become spies can be summed up with the acronym MICE. The letters represent the words *money*, *ideology*, *compromise*, and *ego*. Some people become spies because they are paid well for the information they uncover. Some have a strong belief in their country or in the ideals represented by another country. Others may be compromised, or blackmailed, into spying to avoid punishment or to prevent some dark secret about themselves from being revealed. Still others do it to show off how clever or daring they can be.

Who am I? and *What am I doing here?* Some CIA operatives work under their own names. In spy talk, they are legals—they do their spying while officially working in the American embassy in a foreign country. As U.S. government employees, they can bend some rules of the foreign country without fear of being arrested. If they are caught breaking the law, they are usually sent back to the United States rather than jailed.

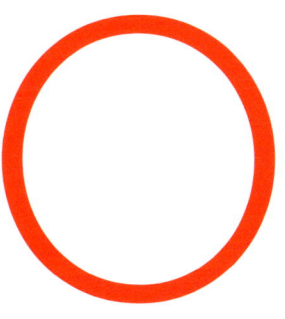ther CIA operatives are classified as illegals—they do their spying using a false name and

a made-up identity. If their cover is blown, the U.S. government will probably deny any knowledge of them or their mission. If they are caught, their punishment is often severe and might include torture or execution.

People who want to become CIA agents don't simply complete an application, undergo classroom and on-the-job-training, and then get sent undercover to a foreign country. It is a long and complicated process. The Company looks for individuals who can deal with "fast-moving, ambiguous, and unstructured situations." In other words, the

CIA wants people who can think on their feet and not get flustered when things go wrong—and things often do go wrong. The agency's website adds, "This requires physical and psychological health, energy, intuition, 'street sense,' and the ability to cope with stress."

The CIA puts its applicants through a series of tough tests: physical, mental, and medical exams; polygraph

Polygraph test

(lie-detector) tests; background checks; and writing tests (most agents spend a lot of time writing reports). Of the 100 or so top recruits in a class, only about 17 make it through the testing. Then the serious training begins.

What kind of training do CIA operatives receive? Former agent Lindsay Moran reveals some of the secrets in her 2005 book *Blowing My Cover* and in a series of online videos. A fairly realistic view of the training is also presented in the 2003 movie *The Recruit*. Operative training takes place at Camp Peary, located near Williamsburg, Virginia. CIA agents call it "The Farm." The course at the Farm includes paramilitary training—martial arts and hand-to-hand combat, use of guns and knives, and field survival techniques. Potential agents learn to drive defensively, to handle speedboats, and to parachute from planes and helicopters. They also endure a "jail sequence." They are put in a cell, deprived of food, water, and sleep, and then interrogated nonstop for nearly two days to test their mental toughness.

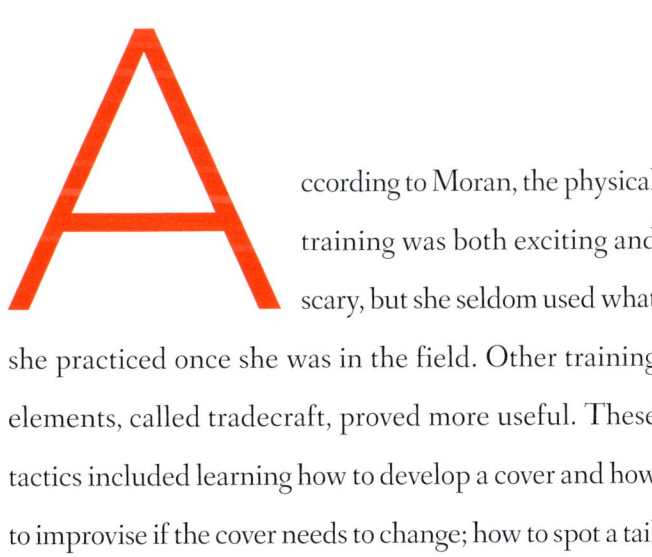

According to Moran, the physical training was both exciting and scary, but she seldom used what she practiced once she was in the field. Other training elements, called tradecraft, proved more useful. These tactics included learning how to develop a cover and how to improvise if the cover needs to change; how to spot a tail

CIA agent Tony Mendez [*left*] meets with U.S. president Jimmy Carter after his successful mission in Iran.

On the Big Screen

In 1979, Islamic **militants** stormed the U.S. Embassy in Tehran, Iran, and took 66 people hostage, holding most of them for 444 days. Six Americans had escaped and were hiding in a Canadian diplomat's home for roughly 80 days. In 1980, CIA agent Tony Mendez snuck into Tehran and pretended to be part of a Canadian group filming a movie. The Americans pretended to be his film crew and used fake paperwork to go through airport security. Once their flight cleared Iranian airspace, the Americans were free. The movie *Argo* is based on this true story.

and avoid being followed; how to use spy cameras, radios and radio detecting devices, and other communication tools. Other tactics included how to mingle comfortably at parties and in the streets; how to set up secret meetings to recruit local **assets**; and how to set up a **drop** for collecting intelligence from assets. Moran says, "You are taught specifically how to spot people who might be potential recruits and how to assess their personality to determine whether or not they might be a good foreign spy. Also, how to seek out their weaknesses . . . that you can prey upon in order to convince them to spy on behalf of the United States." The entire process usually takes more than a year. Then recruits are ready to begin their careers as spies. There is only one catch: They can never tell anyone what they really do for a living.

Early spy cameras could be tough to conceal.

Glove Pistol
Issued by U.S. Navy (ONI), circa 1942 – 1945

Armed with a glove pistol, an ope[rative] still had both hands free. To fire t[he] pistol, the wearer pushed the plu[nger] into an attacker's body.

THE CIA

Tools and Tricks

In spy movies, the heroes often travel on land in high-speed cars equipped with machine guns and rocket boosters. They go airborne via jet packs or flying machines or travel underwater in mini-submarines. They fire guns concealed in briefcases, cufflinks, or umbrellas; attack enemies with shoes fitted with poison tips; make calls from a phone concealed in a shoe; and photograph meetings and documents using the tiniest cameras imaginable. Do real spy gadgets and weapons match those of the movies?

OPPOSITE: Part of a spy museum display

The answer is both yes and no. The CIA's Directorate of Science and Technology (DS&T) is responsible for developing or purchasing gadgets for the agency. Much of the DS&T's budget over the years has been invested in aerial **reconnaissance**—spy planes (crewed and uncrewed), satellites, and the long-range photographic equipment they carry. The Global Hawk is an uncrewed drone that can fly 350 miles (563 kilometers) per hour at altitudes of more than 60,000 feet (18,288 meters) for up to 30 hours straight. Equipped with high-speed cameras and heat-sensing scanners, the Global Hawk can detect anything made of metal on the ground. It has even spotted openings of caves in the mountains of Afghanistan that ground troops missed while searching the area on foot. These planes have proven effective in recognizing enemy military bases and tracking troop movements.

Failure in the Sky

In the mid-1950s, the CIA decided that its agents on the ground could not effectively monitor the growing nuclear capabilities of the Soviet Union. So, the agency ordered construction of the U-2 spy plane, which could fly high enough to avoid detection or attack. In May 1960, U-2 pilot Francis Gary Powers was taking photographs over Soviet territory when an engine failed. The plane dropped to a vulnerable altitude and was struck by Soviet missiles. Powers was thrown from the plane before he could set it to self-destruct. He was captured and tried for espionage in a public trial designed to embarrass the United States.

In 2024, the United States started construction on a new spy plane. The High Accuracy Detection and Exploitation System (HADES) plane will be the first ever to have a cabin like a business jet. However, it will have a lot of technical capabilities that a normal business jet does not. It will operate at higher altitudes and be able to sense deeper and farther than before. This spy plane's focus is on surveillance and reconnaissance.

Over the years, U.S. spy planes have provided vital information but have caused some embarrassment for the country, too. In 1960, for example, a manned U.S. aircraft called the U-2 was shot down while flying illegally within Soviet airspace. The pilot was eventually released as part of a spy exchange, but the plane was never returned.

Modern intelligence work is not just "spy from the sky." Many gadgets developed by the CIA have been designed for use on the ground. These include miniature cameras (using 16-mm film) for photographing secret documents or meetings; electronic listening equipment for eavesdropping, as well as anti-bugging devices to protect Americans from enemy ears; and radios and cipher machines to make sure that communications stay secret. Other gadgets include guns hidden within gloves, cigarette packs, or fountain pens. There are even poison darts.

Some unusual weapons fall into the "dirty tricks" category. For example, a CIA scientist once tried to develop cigars that would poison Cuban **dictator** Fidel Castro when he lit one. The same scientist also formulated special chemicals that, when placed in Castro's boots, would make his hair fall out and embarrass him. Nothing came of these plans, though.

Several gadgets and weapons developed by the DS&T have been controversial— explosives, poisons, nerve gases, chemicals that destroy crops, drugs used as truth serums, and so on. Not everyone agrees that such weaponry is fair to use, even in defending the United States against terrorists. For that reason, some have never been used outside the laboratory.

The types of gadgets and techniques used by U.S. spies have changed over time. For most of history, collecting secret information was done directly by individuals using deception and trickery and a few relatively simple tools. In spy language, this is called HUMINT (human intelligence). A spy involved in HUMINT will usually have several of the following tools on hand: a code book for encoding or decoding messages; a disguise kit containing sunglasses, hair dye, wigs, and hats; a lock pick gun or break-in kit; night-vision goggles to see in the dark; a miniature camera and equipment to convert photos into microdots; and both listening and radio broadcasting equipment.

    Surprisingly, many agents don't carry guns or knives during their day-to-day spy work. Oleg Kalugin, who spied for the Soviet Union in the United States for many years, said, "We never carried weapons in our foreign assignments. Our weapons were our training, our intelligence, and our understanding of what was going on." Kalugin added, if any tools were needed, he was far more likely to use a camera or miniature bugging device than a gun.

    Starting in the 20th century, spies began using various types of technology to help them obtain information. For example, the CIA and other spy agencies gather ELINT

Satellites provide crucial information to the CIA.

(electronic intelligence) via the Internet and through computer monitoring or hacking; COMINT (communication intelligence) by intercepting radio, telephone, and other communications; and PHOTINT (photographic intelligence) by studying photographs taken by spy planes, satellites, or human operatives. All of these methods fall under the heading of TECHINT (technical intelligence). This means that modern spies need a wide range of technical skills and support. Learning to use high-tech gadgets has become an important part of their tradecraft.

Today, it is probably more important for an agent to know how to operate or hack into a computer than how to engage in hand-to-hand combat. Computers can be bugged with a keystroke recorder that can help an agent determine a user's password and duplicate any commands that were previously typed in. Other software, or programs,

Military personnel set up antennae to conduct electronic warfare training exercises.

can be installed to enable an agent to download files for later analysis. With so much information stored digitally these days, it is becoming harder than ever to keep a secret.

The CIA has also found ways to use computers as weapons. For example, during the Gulf War in the early

1990s, CIA computer experts played a trick on Iraqi president Saddam Hussein and his generals. Before the war began in January 1991, they secretly installed a virus—a program that can take over a computer—into a chip built into a printer. A CIA mole working inside Iraq's air defense headquarters in the city of Baghdad hooked up the printer. When war broke out, a signal was sent to activate the virus, which shut down Iraq's defense system in less than a minute. By the time the virus was controlled, many of Iraq's aircraft had been destroyed by United Nations (UN) troops. The CIA also used the Internet to spread false information about UN troop movements during the war, misleading Iraqi military leaders.

THE CIA

Notable Agents

Many exceptional individuals have worked for the CIA since it was founded. Although the secretive nature of the agency means that some agents, especially those working undercover, can never be publicly identified, there are some who can.

OPPOSITE: Dmitri Polyakov was a Soviet general who spied for the CIA during the Cold War, sharing secrets for nearly 25 years before being discovered.

Double agent Oleg Penkovsky [*right*]

During the Cold War between the United States and the Soviet Union, spying and counterespionage efforts intensified. On the American side were the CIA, FBI, and the National Security Agency (NSA); on the Soviet side was the KGB. Both nations put many operatives in the field, recruited assets or moles to spy in their own countries, and did what they could to bribe or turn agents to become double agents. One of the most significant Cold War double agents was high-ranking KGB officer Oleg Penkovsky.

In August 1960, worried that Soviet leader Nikita Khrushchev was going to lead the world into a nuclear war, Penkovsky passed a message to two American tourists on a Moscow bridge and asked them to get it to the CIA. In the message, Penkovsky offered to provide information to U.S. and British intelligence. Over the next two years, Penkovsky hid messages inside candy boxes or placed them into drops,

CIA agent Aldrich Ames

giving the United States and Britain important details about Soviet missile strength and capabilities. Using this information, U.S. president John F. Kennedy was able to confront the Soviets in October 1962 when they were installing missiles in a military headquarters they had established in Cuba. The Soviet Union backed down, and a war was averted. However, Penkovsky was arrested in Moscow and later executed as a **traitor**.

Aldrich Ames is one of the most notorious CIA agents. He was born in Wisconsin and worked his entire career for the CIA. His specialty was to recruit U.S. spies abroad and to discover spies working for the Soviet Union. He became a double agent for the Soviet Union in the mid-1980s, selling intelligence to its KGB. More than 10 CIA agents working inside Russia were executed because of Ames's intelligence. He was paid more than $2.7 million for his information. This is the most money ever paid by Russia or the Soviet Union to any American spy. Ames gave the names of every CIA agent operating in the Soviet Union. He was convicted of espionage and sentenced to life in prison. He is serving his time in Indiana.

Not to be confused with Aldrich Ames, Bob Ames was an American CIA agent known for creating the first-ever clandestine contacts inside the Palestine Liberation Organization (PLO). He rose high in the CIA ranks and was instrumental in developing President Ronald Reagan's Peace Plan. Ames developed assets inside the Mossad (intelligence agency for the State of Israel), PLO, and all across the Middle East. His assets and relationships were built on trust, rather than force or cunning. His most important contacts, Salameh and Zein, were never paid by the CIA. This was a different approach, making Ames stand out in his spycraft. Tragically, he was killed when a car bomb exploded at the U.S. Embassy in Beirut, Lebanon, in 1982. The explosion killed 17 Americans and 7 other CIA agents. Many in the intelligence industry wonder if Ames had lived longer, would the CIA have had better intelligence in the Middle East? Instead, a vacuum in Middle Eastern intelligence was created when the bomb went off.

Women have played key roles in U.S. intelligence—even before the CIA was founded. In 1941, Adelaide

Hawkins became an assistant cryptographic (data-coding) clerk for the OSS. She also was one of the first women ever to work in espionage. The OSS created its first spy network during World War II, and Hawkins oversaw the agency's message center in Washington, D.C. Her specialty was working with ciphers. She trained spies working behind enemy lines on how to communicate.

U.S. Embassy in Beirut after the 1982 bombing

When the CIA was founded in 1947, Hawkins was one of the agency's highest-ranking women, along with Virginia Hall. Hall was the CIA's first female paramilitary officer. She did clandestine work behind enemy lines during World War II and the Cold War. Even though she was missing her left leg below the knee, she was still instrumental in organizing agent networks and helping prisoners of war escape. The secret police of Nazi Germany called her "The Limping Lady" and tried desperately to catch her. She was well known for her exceptional spycraft and received the Trailblazer award in 2022.

Barbara Sude worked as an analyst for the CIA. She wrote the famous brief for U.S. president George W. Bush on August 6, 2001, warning that Al-Qaeda wanted to attack the United States. She ended up being correct when Al-Qaeda attacked the World Trade Center just over a month later, on September 11.

Many women have played integral parts in analyzing intelligence and working in the field for the CIA. They've served as case officers, station managers, and more. In 2018, Gina Haspel became the first female director of the agency.

THE CIA

On a Mission

Following World War II, American intelligence agencies turned to dealing with the rise of communism around the world. The CIA's Cold War-era operations were designed to help overthrow communist-leaning governments and place in power governments that would be more supportive of U.S. political and business interests.

OPPOSITE: Rebel groups, such as Nicaragua's Contras, received financial assistance from the CIA in the 1980s to help them overthrow their socialist government.

In 1947, for example, CIA operatives used money and **propaganda** to stop the Italian Communist Party from winning national elections. In 1954, CIA agents helped military leaders in Guatemala overthrow that country's pro-communist president.

The most controversial CIA operations were those carried out in the powerful, oil-producing country of Iran. In 1953, the shah, or king, of Iran was pushed out of power, and a newly elected government took over. British and U.S. oil companies had major wells and plants in Iran, and the new prime minister threatened to nationalize these. Western leaders worried that Iran might cut off oil to Britain and the United States or raise prices significantly. The CIA supported the efforts of Iranians who overthrew the new government and brought the shah back to power. Over the next 25 years, the shah

CIA Seal

The CIA seal is frequently used in an official manner. It appears on the lobby floor of the CIA's headquarters and is used on badges, vehicles, letterhead, and all kinds of communications. The seal uses symbols that represent the agency:

eagle—the official bird of the United States; well known for its strength, sight, and speed
shield—shows that the CIA works to defend the country against attack
16-point star—like a compass, representing intelligence coming in from every part of the world

ruled with an iron hand, often oppressing his people. Still, CIA advisers continued to train the shah's secret police to help him hold power. Then, in 1979, these secret police turned on the shah. A new government took over in Iran, led by a radical Muslim religious leader known as the Ayatollah Khomeini. Since that time, the Iranian and U.S. governments have often clashed.

In 1959, the CIA began to focus on a new problem—a communist dictatorship established by Fidel Castro 90 miles (145 km) from Florida on the island of Cuba. Many Cubans who opposed Castro fled to the United States and began making plans to overthrow the dictator and reestablish a democracy in their homeland. The CIA was eager to support them. So, in April 1961, an attack force of 1,500 Cubans, with CIA help, sailed from Nicaragua to the Bay of Pigs in southern Cuba, where they planned to land and start a revolution. Unfortunately, Castro had been warned about the attack, and his air force and ground troops wiped out the attackers, capturing nearly 1,200 and killing another 100. The U.S. government was forced to deal with Castro for the release of the prisoners and eventually agreed to pay Cuba $53 million in food and supplies.

Terrorist activities in the 1990s and 2000s have forced the U.S. intelligence community to act with new focus, both inside and outside the country. On September 11, 2001, members of Al-Qaeda hijacked four passenger jets and used them in coordinated terrorist attacks on the United States. Two of the planes crashed into the Twin Towers of the World Trade Center in New York City. Another plane was flown into the Pentagon in Arlington County, Virginia. The fourth plane crashed in Pennsylvania when the passengers revolted against the hijackers

OPPOSITE After being struck by airplanes on 9/11, the twin towers of the World Trade Center collapsed.

and prevented it from crashing into its intended target. Almost 3,000 people lost their lives in the 9/11 attacks.

The CIA's New York office was destroyed on 9/11. While first responders and firefighters were rescuing people, the CIA was sifting through rubble trying to find classified documents. The agency claims that the terrorists were unaware of the location of the CIA office, but it's unknown what the terrorists knew. On the evening of September 11, President George W. Bush stated, "The search is underway for those who are behind these evil acts. I've directed the full resources of our intelligence and law enforcement communities to find those responsible and bring them to justice." He then declared a "War on Terror," and the CIA launched a campaign against Al-Qaeda.

The CIA embarked on an exhaustive search for Al-Qaeda members and leaders. It created a network of "black sites" to interrogate and extract information from suspected terrorists, and then it used this information to hunt down leaders. Many people in the United States, including lawmakers, disagreed with the CIA's tactics. An investigation was started and a report filed with the U.S. Justice Department.

How could the CIA have missed such a colossal terrorist plan? The public and government officials called for answers. The 9/11 Commission Report was created. It took four years of combing through data and interviewing agents, policymakers, and employees in all intelligence agencies. One major finding of the report was that the FBI, CIA, and other agencies didn't share information and prevented decision-makers from "connecting the dots." In 2004, the Intelligence and Terrorism Prevention Act created a new office called the Office of the Director of National Intelligence (ODNI).

The ODNI would oversee 17 intelligence agencies. In the past, the CIA reported to the President. Today it reports to the ODNI.

In 2021, Ukraine started the process of applying to the North Atlantic Treaty Organization (NATO). NATO is a military alliance established in 1949. Its key principle is a "collective defense." This means if one of its members is attacked, it is considered an attack on all NATO members, and the other members will come to that country's aid. Ukraine had just witnessed Russia take over Crimea, a part of Ukraine. Within weeks of Ukraine applying for NATO membership, Russia sent thousands of troops to the shared border. For months, more and more troops gathered at the border and conducted what the Russians said were "training exercises."

The Hunt Ends

For nine years following the 9/11 terrorist attacks on the United States, Osama bin Laden, the mastermind behind the attacks, hid. Then, in the fall of 2010, CIA agents in Pakistan located bin Laden's likely hiding place near the city of Abbottabad. They observed the building carefully for many months. Then, on May 1, 2011, U.S. president Barack Obama gave the go-ahead for an attack. In a daring 40-minute raid early in the morning of May 2, a team of Navy SEALs broke into the building, found bin Laden, and killed him. They took his body, gathered vital papers and tapes stored in his room, and quickly flew out of Pakistan.

Five years earlier, in 2016, the CIA had started training elite Ukrainian commando forces and spies that operated in Russia and across Europe. The CIA shared intelligence with Ukraine of Russian president Vladimir Putin's plans to attack. CIA agents remained in Ukraine even after U.S. personnel were evacuated in January 2022. The CIA released details of Russian troops and warned that Russia would invade, but the world didn't listen. In February 2022, Russia sent what they described as "peace keeping" forces into Ukraine. The move escalated into a full-blown invasion, with artillery and missile attacks. The CIA agents still in Ukraine were able to provide critical intelligence of where Russia was planning strikes and what weapons systems were being used. Without their help, the Russian takeover would have been swift. As of August 2024, Ukraine was

Ukraine continues to fight Russian aggression with the aid of the United States, the CIA, and NATO.

continuing to fight off Russia's invasion with help from CIA intelligence and its Western allies.

On October 7, 2023, Hamas terrorists and Palestinian militants surprised the world by attacking a concert and civilian area in Israel. The militants killed and kidnapped hundreds of civilians. They attacked from the Gaza Strip, which is a small strip of land that has been fought over by many countries. For decades, conflict in the Gaza/Israel region has been considered routine. On September 28, the CIA received warning that the Hamas group was ready to launch rockets into Israel over the course of the next several days. A second warning came on October 5. It also warned of violence and probable attacks. These warnings were days before the deadly events of October 7. Many people wonder why the warnings were never communicated to U.S. president Joe Biden or Israel. The CIA and Israeli intelligence were tracking Hamas and expected the attack to be just another round of small-scale violence. Unfortunately, they were wrong this time, and many people suffered for it.

The CIA specializes in secrecy. Whether its agents are trying to uncover or undermine terrorists in the Middle East or helping the United States deal with hostile political regimes around the world, the CIA's missions are vital to U.S. security. Every day, CIA agents operate in 130 countries on 6 different continents. They are committed to protecting Americans from threats of all kinds. And most do so without ever receiving public recognition for their service.

Selected Bibliography

Arkin, William M. "Exclusive: The CIA's Blind Spot about the Ukraine War." *Newsweek*. July 5, 2023. https://www.newsweek.com/2023/07/21/exclusive-cias-blind-spot-about-ukraine-war-1810355.html.

Bamford, James. *Body of Secrets: Anatomy of the Ultra-Secret National Security Agency: From the Cold War through the Dawn of a New Century.* New York: Doubleday, 2001.

Bird, Kai. *The Good Spy: The Life and Death of Robert Ames.* New York: Crown Publishers, 2014.

Crowdy, Terry. *The Enemy Within: A History of Espionage.* Oxford; New York: Osprey, 2006.

Hutchinson, Bill. "Israel-Hamas War: Timeline and Key Developments." ABC News Network. November 22, 2023. https://abcnews.go.com/International/timeline-surprise-rocket-attack-hamas-israel/story?id=103816006.

Moran, Lindsay. *Blowing My Cover: My Life as a CIA Spy*. New York: G. P. Putnam's Sons, 2005.

Mundy, Liza. *The Sisterhood: The Secret History of Women at the CIA*. New York: Crown, 2023.

Priest, Dana, and William M. Arkin. "A Hidden World, Growing Beyond Control." *The Washington Post*. July 19, 2010. https://www.washingtonpost.com/investigations/top-secret-america/2010/07/19/hidden-world-growing-beyond-control-2.

Glossary

agent	a person who works for, but is not necessarily officially employed by, an intelligence service
asset	a hidden source acting as a spy or providing secret information to a spy
cipher	a message in code
clandestine	secretive
Cold War	the hostile competition between the United States and its allies against the Soviet Union and its allies that began at the end of World War II and lasted until the collapse of the Soviet Union in 1991
communism	a political and economic system in which all goods and property are owned by the state and shared by all members of the public
counterespionage	efforts made by a nation's intelligence agency to catch and eliminate spies working against the country and protect the country against sabotage or terrorism
covert	undercover or hidden
dictator	one who rules with absolute power, often in an oppressive way

double agent	a spy for one country who doubles as a spy for a second country and often provides false information to the first country
drop	a prearranged spot for dropping off and picking up information gathered through spying
espionage	the act of spying
intelligence	information uncovered and transmitted by a spy
intercept	to stop, take, or interrupt something while it's in process or moving from point A to point B
militant	a person who is aggressively engaged in a cause
mole	an employee of one intelligence service who actually works for another service or who works undercover in a foreign country to supply intelligence
operative	an undercover agent working for an intelligence agency
propaganda	material distributed to promote a government's or group's point of view or to damage an opposing point of view; some propaganda is untrue or unfairly exaggerated
reconnaissance	spying activities
recruit	to hire or enlist
traitor	a person who betrays another's trust or is false to one's duty or country

Websites

The International Spy Museum
https://www.spymuseum.org
Explore frequently asked questions about spying and bios of real-life agents.

National Cryptologic Museum
https://www.nsa.gov/museum
Find out more about America's history of cryptology and take a virtual tour.

The World Factbook
https://www.cia.gov/the-world-factbook
Take a look at how the CIA sees the world.

Index

9/11, 65, 67, 68, 70
Al-Qaeda, 27, 58, 59, 65, 67, 68
Ames, Aldrich, 54–55
Ames, Bob, 55–56
assets, 36, 53, 56
Beirut embassy bombing, 56, 57
Berg, Moe, 20
Bush, George W., 58, 67
Camp Peary ("The Farm"), 32
Castro, Fidel, 43, 64, 65
Child, Julia, 20
cipher machines, 10, 13, 43
Cold War, 17, 51, 53, 58, 61
Cooper, Merian, 20
counterespionage, 15, 53
cover stories, 26, 33
Crypto AG, 10
Cuba, 54, 64, 65
divisions of the CIA
   Directorate of Intelligence, 22
   Directorate of Science and
      Technology, 22, 40, 44
   Directorate of Support, 22–23
   National Clandestine Service, 22, 23
Donovan, William "Wild Bill," 17, 18, 19, 20
double agents, 17, 23, 27, 53, 55
Federal Bureau of Investigation (FBI), 15, 17, 53, 68
first American intelligence agency, 15
Ford, John, 20
Germany, 10, 13, 16, 20, 58
Hall, Virginia, 58
Hamas, 74, 75
Haspel, Gina, 59
Hawkins, Adelaide, 57, 58
headquarters, 23, 63
hostages, 35
Hussein, Saddam, 49
illegal spies, 29–30
Iran, 35, 62, 64
Israel, 56, 74, 75
Japan, 16, 18, 20

Kalugin, Oleg, 45
KGB, 53, 55
legal spies, 29
Mendez, Tony, 34, 35
moles, 17, 23, 49, 53
Moran, Lindsay, 32, 33
movies and TV shows, 25, 26, 32, 35, 39
Nicaragua, 61, 64
Office of Strategic Services (OSS), 17, 18, 20, 57
Office of the Director of National Intelligence, 69
Operation Rubicon, 13
Penkovsky, Oleg, 52, 53–54
PLO, 55, 56
Polyakov, Dmitri, 51
Powers, Francis Gary, 41
reasons for spying, 28
Russia, 55, 69, 72, 73, 74
seal, 63
Signal Intelligence Service (SIS), 16, 17
Soviet Union, 17, 18, 41, 45, 53, 54, 55
Storm, Morten, 27
Sude, Barbara, 58
Sun Tzu, 9
tools of the trade
   cameras, 22, 36, 37, 39, 40, 43, 45
   computers, 45, 47–49
   disguises, 25, 44
   drones, 6, 40
   gadgets, 9, 22, 39, 40, 42, 43, 44, 47
   polygraphs, 12, 31
   satellites, 22, 40, 46, 47
   spy planes, 22, 40, 41, 42, 47
   weapons, 26, 32, 39, 43, 44, 45
tradecraft, 33, 36, 47
training, 30, 31–33, 36
Truman, Harry, 18
Ukraine, 69, 72, 73, 74
Washington, George, 15
World War I, 17
World War II, 16, 17, 18, 20, 57, 58, 61